The Elephant Is Sprinting!

*Attracting, Managing, and Retaining the
Next Generation of Talent in India*

ARUN BAHARANI

Copyright © 2016 Arun Baharani.

All rights reserved. No part of this book may be reproduced, stored, or transmitted by any means—whether auditory, graphic, mechanical, or electronic—without written permission of both publisher and author, except in the case of brief excerpts used in critical articles and reviews. Unauthorized reproduction of any part of this work is illegal and is punishable by law.

ISBN: 978-1-4834-5555-6 (sc)
ISBN: 978-1-4834-5556-3 (e)

Library of Congress Control Number: 2016912030

Because of the dynamic nature of the Internet, any web addresses or links contained in this book may have changed since publication and may no longer be valid. The views expressed in this work are solely those of the author and do not necessarily reflect the views of the publisher, and the publisher hereby disclaims any responsibility for them.

Any people depicted in stock imagery provided by Thinkstock are models, and such images are being used for illustrative purposes only.
Certain stock imagery © Thinkstock.

Lulu Publishing Services rev. date: 9/26/2016

In honor and memory of my parents, Lavina and Bob

Happiness comes when your work and words
are of benefit to yourself and others.
—Buddha

Acknowledgments

I would like to thank my friends and colleagues for their inspiration and guidance in the creation of this book.

Gina Fitch, my muse, my mentor, my guide. Your patience, kindness, and editing advice from the onset helped me write a book that makes me proud. Jayshree Nathoo, you've stood by my side as a good friend through thick and thin. You gave me strength when I couldn't see tomorrow. Your love has been the greatest gift anyone could ever ask for in a lifetime.

To the global Fortune 500 leaders I've had the pleasure of working with throughout my career, thank you for sharing your insights and brilliant advice. To my clients, thank you for inviting me into your workplace worlds and giving me the opportunity to share my experiences with you. To my former teammates at CNN and the Walt Disney Company who inspired me to venture down the road of management consulting. Logan Burton, Justin Scholfield, Carolyn Lockridge and the entire team at Lulu Publishing, I thank you for your hard work and dedication for the publication of my work.

Contents

Introduction xiii
CHAPTER 1   I Am Global. 1
CHAPTER 2   The Digital Generation 7
CHAPTER 3   Indian Corporate Structure 17
CHAPTER 4   Managing Attrition. 23
CHAPTER 5   Virtual Engagement 29
CHAPTER 6   Say Again? 35
CHAPTER 7   Coaching for Success 41
CHAPTER 8   Work-Life Balance. 47
CHAPTER 9   Managing Time Zones. 53
CHAPTER 10   The Hyper-Connected World 57
CHAPTER 11   The Virtual Workspace 61
CHAPTER 12   Your First Step 65
Endnotes 67

Introduction

As a global leadership consultant and coach for Fortune 500 companies since 2001, the managers of teams in India I work with constantly say they're so busy they have little time for skill-building opportunities. Their top concerns include how to boost productivity, what to do to effectively retain top performers, and how to motivate their teams. Based on what I've been told and what I've observed, a manager's guide detailing practical solutions for these and other core people-management challenges in India is in high demand—or should be. Today's manager is working at the speed of light, juggling new and ever-changing technologies, corporate processes, and expectations of senior management. With limited personal time in today's demanding work environments, the last thing on a manager's mind is sitting down with a bulky book on how to effectively manage and motivate his or her talent in India. This handbook is specifically designed for the manager on the go. It is practical, short, precise, and beginning in chapter 3, includes comprehensive checklists that focus on what leaders should have on their radars when managing the next generation entering their workforce in India.

My dedication to global consulting work was jump-started when I was a leader for a division of the Walt Disney Company. One of the most valuable leadership-training experiences I encountered as a manager at Disney was one of their management training programs for onboarding newly appointed leaders. The guidance I received in the weeklong training program, which included the tactical steps for building trust, rewarding employees, and recognizing staff, eventually became the cornerstone of my Disney career in operations management. Those insights definitely impacted the success I've achieved as a consultant designing international management coaching programs for Fortune 500 companies, including auto manufacturers, banking institutions, pharmaceutical entities, information technology, and international manufacturing firms.

There are many factors that led to my consulting work in assisting companies to attract, manage, and retain talent specifically in India. In the 1990s, India's economic reforms and a reduction of state regulations accelerated the country toward a free market model. Suddenly, India became a top offshore location for partnerships in various industries, including information technology, engineering, and manufacturing. Globally dispersed teams were suddenly challenged with managing geographic distances, time zone hurdles, language barriers, limited face time, and rapidly evolving communication technologies.

Now, the landscape is once again changing. Currently the employment of young, just-out-of-college workers in India has created a new challenge for leaders. There is a gap between the employment expectations of this new tech-savvy generation and previous generations. Young professionals in India have new definitions for what it means to be employed by an organization, how to engage with an organization, and how they hope to be empowered and motivated. What is critical to state is presently psychologists, demographers, and trend spotters are witnessing the dramatic influences this new digital generation is making at the workplace. This is not the first time supervisors have had to adjust to generational differences in the workplace. For example, in the United States, each generation has brought different motivators and expectations: traditionalists (prior to 1946) expected employment security and retirement rewards, baby boomers (1946–1964) were motivated by status and recognition; Gen Xers (1965–1984) were driven by self-improvement and career security versus job security; and Gen Yers (1984–2004) have their own set of unique expectations.[1] Socioeconomic factors are creating a similar shift in the Indian workforce. In India, job security is no longer the only relevant factor to this generation. They are motivated by personal development, mobile careers, personal flexibility, and accelerated leadership programs. The once slow-moving, bureaucratic Indian socioeconomic system of decades past is now catapulting into the twenty-first century. Stereotypes are dying. A key catalyst for change is the youth who are darting toward a future filled with a desire to influence and overhaul the status quo. The elephant, my friends, is sprinting.

By the year 2025, young workers are expected to make up 75 percent of the global workforce.[2] This means we should probably be paying attention to some of the shifting demographics across the globe. That is the focus of my recent consulting work. I've come across a tremendous amount of research about entry-level employees in the West but limited data on the influence of the growing digital generation abroad. I believe the impact the young workforce on India's business landscape is going to be truly significant in the next decade and must be a focus for leadership.

Today's leader needs to adjust to global generational expectations. Corporate mandates are being enacted to adhere to these changing trends like how Colgate-Palmolive is "encouraging a healthy balance between work and personal responsibilities," as stated on the company's career page.[3] IBM has an employee "Well-Being Management System" program with flexible work schedules.[4] Samsung has implemented cutting-edge designs for global work spaces to foster communication and innovation.[5] It is essential to shift to accommodate new generations joining the workforce. Recognizing that now versus later will be the difference between leaders being ahead of the game or having to play catch-up. For example, in February 2015, *Harvard Business Review* published an article discussing *why* it's important to consider global millennial expectations and needs, but few, to my knowledge, have come up with concrete recommendations for *how* a manager should deal with shifting expectations of the next generation of workers.[6] I have written this book to share with managers my recommendations for the necessary tactical daily adjustments they must consider to adapt to the latest generational trends in India.

This handbook is derived from qualitative discussions with clients who are managers at Fortune 500 companies, quantitative publicized research data, surveys, observations, and interviews with young employees from India. Each chapter reflects the most significant topics in attracting, managing, and retaining entry-level talent. I have incorporated my insights via a checklist system that will allow you to review and verify that you're addressing necessary steps for attracting and maintaining your high performers in India.

1 I Am Global

Technology continues to saturate our everyday personal and work lives. Information is catapulting nonstop into our devices at lightning speed. We all know this because we're experiencing it firsthand. Many of us are managing work and personal obligations from our smartphones practically every minute of every day. A growing number of us with global teams and employees are managing employee expectations, facilitating performance reviews, and coaching on conflict-related issues with staff we've never even met face to face.

When managing staff overseas, who's got time for sleep? Is this an exaggeration? Not really, since it is the reality for many of the international managers I advise and coach in cities across the globe.

The global village is no longer a faraway concept. It's been a part of our lives for quite some time now. Before we delve into this topic, here is an important statement all managers should consider: "I am global." Read it out loud to yourself. How does that statement make you feel? Are you comfortable with the fact that the business world we live in is no longer contained within one office or country? If your company's international presence has been critical for your organization's growth and survival, then are you effectively leveraging your global partnerships? Are you developing skills to build trust and manage in an international environment? Do you know and understand the business expectations of your incoming staff, business partners, and vendors in India?

The truth is, in a global economy, we can't afford to be parochial. Borders of time and space have long dissipated, and virtual collaboration is the everyday reality. How we embrace international business will have a significant impact on our ability as managers to not only survive in the changing corporate landscape but to strive in it. The depth and range of our global mind-set will influence our outcomes, and that is especially true in regard to managing the next generation of digitally hyper-connected workers. The percentage of us who do not embrace globalization may still be thinking, *I wish I didn't have to work with offshore teams in India. I am going to just go through the motions and hope it goes away one day soon.* These are statements I've heard when coaching on the skills required to lead teams in India today.

Global connectivity is a part of practically every manager's business DNA. It is common for a manager to have geographically dispersed matrix teams in different time zones with limited face time. But, surprisingly, our research indicates that not all companies are thinking about how the new generation of workers in regions like India are impacting the process of hiring, managing, and retaining top performers.

Companies in the United States have been spending a lot of time trying to figure out how to attract and develop their own domestic workforce, but they are quickly realizing that the on-boarding and engagement of incoming staff members in other regions across the globe has gotten just as complex. In my experience, the new generation of workers across the globe is more similar than different, regardless of geographic boundaries, due to their coming up in the digital age. Digital is the bond that links the next-generation employee, and it doesn't matter whether that employee sits in Chicago or Bangalore. Within today's fast-paced, technology-driven environments, global managers are working with an emerging young and savvy generation of "digital natives—the only generation for which [the Internet, mobile technology, and social media] are not something they've had to adapt to."[7] This hyper-connected generation is less defined by national origin, identity, or corporate culture and more influenced by the technologically intertwined and borderless collective cyber whole.

Research my firm Arun Baharani Consulting has conducted with United States- and European-based organizations indicates that using the "dump-and-run" approach to managing global work and teams in India is outdated and no longer sustainable. We define the dump-and-run model as the 24/7 turnaround where a team may be sending work or tasks at the end of your workday to your offshore in India and expecting it to be completed and sitting in your inbox the next morning. The top reason it's not working is because India's corporate environment has matured. Employees there have had a couple of decades of technology-driven virtual partnerships with Western organizations. The workforce, which at one time had limited international management skills, is globally savvy and for the most part acculturated to international management standards. The teams I work with today in India have asserted their place in global business.

Tom, an IT project manager I recently interviewed said the following:

> When we first learned that my IT (information technology) project team would be working with our company's location in India, we thought we'd just send them work at the end of our day and expect the work back in the morning. That's how we did it for years. But it's not working anymore because the employees in India expect more out of their jobs now. Younger team members want to be directly involved throughout the process. And they actually want more challenging work. In many ways, they are no different than the employees I work in the United States. Furthermore, they want to be viewed as part of our team and not as a separate work group confined by geographic boundaries.

Exposure to the international workplace has boosted self-esteem and created more confident behaviors among global employees in corporate environments. In India, a young, out-of-college engineer is no longer going to rejoice just because an international organization recruited him or her.

Employees are aware of their worth and have been aggressively negotiating lucrative sign-on packages. All of this employee confidence has dramatically impacted the definition of loyalty and retaining high performers.

Keeping up with generational changes regarding loyalty, retention, and working through fast-paced technological challenges—including time zones and communication misunderstandings—are the realities of today's managers. Here are three examples to highlight these obstacles:

- A senior engineer with a manufacturing company came to me with concerns about managing his team at a site in Gurgaon. He had four technology employees who he thought he could meet with once a week via conference call. That was how he expected to touch base on project progress, but he found that his employees wanted to have frequent discussions about developing their technical skills. "They're looking for training opportunities, and they want my help in determining their career paths. Meanwhile, I sit in Chicago. How do I find the time?" I suggested scheduling one-on-one coaching sessions with each of his team members on a quarterly basis and presenting a structured employee-development plan with an actionable timetable for training and personal growth opportunities.

- A manager of finance with a banking institution in New York City noticed a significant shift in expectations from her team in India. Her full-time employees wanted to grow their careers at lightning speed. Many were demanding promotions every six months, which was an unrealistic expectation given the company's compensation structure. Since her company's attrition rate was at about 25 percent in India, staff retention was one of her biggest concerns. She wanted to know how she could effectively manage all the expectations, especially from the new generation of her team hires. I recommended understanding the personal and cultural implications of promotions in India. For many employees, promotions are perceived as the passage to societal acceptance by one's family and peers. The ability to gain status in one's community via a promotion at work can determine one's fate in how the person is respected, accepted, and honored. My recommendation was that she encourage her employees to develop managerial skills through training programs and assign them to projects that would allow them to showcase their strengths and help them build long-term career growth plans.

- An IT project manager in Palo Alto stated, "My project team sits in India. They tell me that they are surprised and frustrated because they're not being given sufficient ever-changing and cutting-edge technical skills and leadership-development training opportunities." I suggested coaching his teams to research inter-company training opportunities and providing guidance on off-site learning programs or seminars for building relevant technical skills and management competencies.

These are typical examples of the sudden new challenges of a twenty-first-century global manager with direct reports in India. Do any of these examples sound like the world you live in? You might be asking, "How should a global leader be preparing for this new wave of employees in India? What should be at the forefront of our minds—and what steps should we consider—in managing productivity and healthy work environments?" I'll explore these questions in the following chapters.

The Digital Generation

I've encountered four traits in employees that managers might not be in tune with. Young workers in India consider different factors than previous generations did when negotiating their contracts, and these factors should be on your radar. If you're going to be interviewing and hiring the new generation of out-of-college employees entering the workforce, you may be faced with these traits.

I won't be stereotyped.

There was a time when most employees in India would be silent on conference calls because in a traditional, hierarchical business culture, only the person with authority speaks for the team. This is an example of a generalization that is quickly dissipating in many industries. The archaic paradigm of measuring an individual's international business savvy by "country stereotypes" is no longer fully applicable.

As a CNN newsroom staff member and protocol attaché to Ted Turner, Judy Woodruff, and Larry King, I advised on the basic etiquette of how to bow with government and business leaders from Asia and when to kiss on both cheeks if meeting dignitaries from certain European countries. That's still applicable today if you work with the US State Department, but it's definitely not necessary when you're talking about skills for managing a global workforce. The last couple decades of global collaboration have created a significant increase of "the internationally savvy employee" in India. These astute employees have the dexterity to successfully operate within multiple business settings across time zones and continents. The young workforce I meet in Chennai, Mumbai, and Bangalore are a new generation that is influenced by global business, media, and connectivity. Many in the middle class are experiencing higher living standards than their parents, are very well paid, well traveled, entrepreneurial, and independent—and that's how they want to be viewed.

This sociological phenomenon is driven by the shifts in demographics in India. By 2020, India will be the world's youngest country, with the average age of around twenty-nine.[8] The portion of these young citizens living in large cities like Bangalore, Mumbai, Chennai, and New Delhi are fully aware of the behaviors required for global business standards. A significant portion of this emerging group are empowered women who are changing the landscape of a traditionally male-dominated corporate culture. Women have made significant inroads in professional sectors. For example, while women only lead one in ten companies, more than half of those are in the financial sector, including top public and private banks.[9] Compared to a worldwide rate of 3 percent, 11.7 percent of India's 5,100 pilots are women.[10]

When discussing the dangers of stereotypes in virtual environments with a team of engineers at a conference in New York City, I received feedback from a participant from India. He lived in Mumbai and worked as an electrical engineer for an international manufacturing corporation. He studied at universities in India and the United States and felt his internship in New York City gave him the necessary insight for working effectively within a Western corporate setting. He gained the necessary skills to successfully handle global assignments with virtual teams. He said, "I speak and understand the global language of business, and my behaviors should not be stereotyped just because I am Indian and am based in India."

One of the greatest mistakes of managing tomorrow's global workforce would be to stereotype the younger generations based on a country's culture. What may have been traditionally typical a decade ago continues to have less relevance as onboarding of technologically sophisticated employees continues to broaden. Today, employees in corporate environments are empowered by leaders who are more prone to ensuring that their teams are aligned with the global rules of engagement.

One way to avoid stereotyping an entire country or staff is to begin looking at your India partners as individual contributors. Each member has to be viewed as a distinct individual with a unique set of personal values, skills, talents, and global competencies. As a manager, one cookie-cutter approach to managing all your employees is not going to be effective. In today's global environment, it is a requirement for managers to take the time and make the effort to get to know each of their Indian employees on an individual level. This will give you a sense of what managerial approaches you'll need to take with each of your staff members.

I'm loyal to myself.

The definition of global employee loyalty has shifted, especially since the recent back-to-back recessions. Many across generational lines in the workforce are skeptical, and others have given up on defining a career as lifetime employment. A report from MillennialBranding.com found that 60 percent of Millennials in the United States are typically not staying at a job for more than three years.[11] They are being defined as "detach-ees." For this generation, institutions are subordinate to individual needs.[12] From my observations, how leaders develop and groom key employees is vital to successfully managing employees with the "self-loyalty" mind-set.

In India, the young generation of workers is no longer as concerned with giving themselves over to the organization. Don't get me wrong. That is happening—but only when they feel it's a right fit. Until then, they are happy to risk jumping from organization to organization. Today's employees have grown up with the ability to create branding for themselves in a way that previous generations did not. Just as this is the digital generation, it is the social media generation. LinkedIn and Twitter profiles may be a part of employees' identities, contributing to their personal branding and the ownership of workplace individuality. Personal branding is fueling the need for employees to develop their own personal identities within organizations. From my observations, employees today are asking, "Are my managers willing to take the time to help me develop my business strengths? And are they willing to support my long-term career goals through coaching and training initiatives?"

A senior executive with a company in London participated in one of my recent seminars. She knew that her geographically dispersed team members were not going to be loyal to the organization if she and other leaders did not make the initiative to be loyal to them. She said, "For them to stick around, I have to personally make a concerted effort for face time. I have to build a personal connection." She had to find time to engage with her virtual employees and demonstrate her loyalty to them in order to not lose her high performers to the competitors.

To avoid losing your employees to start-ups and entrepreneurial ventures, have you as an organization considered personal entrepreneurial developmental opportunities to motivate, engage, and—most importantly—retain your staff? To manage loyalty, organizations are spending time and resources to explore sustainable solutions that allow people to develop their individual unique skills and strengths.

From 2010 to 2015, I coached Fortune 500 companies with operations in India and came to several conclusions. An employee is not loyal to an organization; an employee is loyal to his or her manager. Relationships with individual managers influence loyalty and trust more than organizations do. In India, the importance and respect for family permeates from the home to the office. A manager is treated as an older sibling to give guidance and direction, and it's not unusual for peers in an organization to join in each other's family events. Research indicates that a manager's ability to coach and develop an employee's individual management and technical skills heavily influences the employee's decision to stay or leave the organization. The leaders at the various organizations I interviewed initiated coaching and career-development programs to retain their best performers. Here are some sample initiatives:

- *Information technology firm in Bangalore*: An engineering division initiated a mentoring program for high-performing employees. Once a month, employees could have an informal "question-and-answer" call with a director from one of the company's global engineering locations.

- *Banking institution in Mumbai*: As part of its core employee-loyalty initiatives, the bank established an employee-recognition program spearheaded by divisional senior leadership. Every quarter, one member from each division was recognized with an award and monetary bonus for his or her innovative client solutions.

- *Automotive company in Gurgaon*: As part of a its global talent-development initiative, the organization encouraged leaders to seek and pick technically advanced talent for cross-functional teams for short-term (three-to-six-month) assignments in other parts of the world.

When it comes to staff retention, the reality is that a company can no longer just do what it does—it has to consider strategies to appeal. These leaders understood the need for talent-management systems, and their leadership initiatives prioritized talent growth. However, for these initiatives to have maintained momentum, the leaders who started them, had to play significant roles in facilitating and maintaining the processes. Two out of the three above mentioned recommendations are low cost and can have immediate impacts and returns. However, if you plan to implement these types of initiatives, you'll need leadership commitment and dedicated time and resources.

I require more than a paycheck.

Money is a determining factor for the new generation of employees entering the workplace, but it is not necessarily the driving force. A decade ago, an employee in India would work for a well-respected company for low pay and be content that he or she worked for a prestigious international organization.

An Economist Intelligence Unit study entitled "Global Firms in 2020: The Next Generation of Change for Organizations and Workers" found that from those industry-wide global employees surveyed, the critical criteria for job satisfaction beyond compensation included:[13]

- opportunities for continued learning
- short-term international work assignments
- career planning
- coaching and mentoring

Leaders are going to have to allocate more time to understanding the goals and aspirations of their overseas teams. The steps you should consider to accomplish this goal include:

- *Create global coaching moments.* Coaching employees does not necessarily have to take up a large amount of time. Engaging your staff in quick, coachable moments can be just as impactful. A brief, one-on-one conversation after a conference call to discuss meeting outcomes is an example of a coachable moment.

- *Promote learning and career-building opportunities.* Identifying team strengths and providing feedback on where they can improve is a good approach to helping your people understand their advancement goals. Suggest training courses and off-site programs that are fitting for your staff members and their individual career paths.

- *Encourage innovation and creativity.* Special departmental projects are a good way to get your employees involved in creative thinking and spark innovation. Select talent that you think would benefit from special projects. For example, ask members of your engineering team to measure how technological tools are impacting global productivity. After collecting data, the team would present an innovative plan to leadership outlining how to improve productivity with technology.

I'm experiencing burnout.

Work-life balance continues to be a contentious topic in corporate settings. Managers I interview are always eager to share their perspectives. Some find it has a positive impact, and others see it as a hindrance to productivity. Many think the terminology is skewed. Is it realistic to strive for work-life balance? Today, is it more about trying to fit in life around work?

A manager I interviewed stated, "I'm in San Francisco, I take 5:00 a.m. calls with Mumbai every weekday, and then I have to attend back-to-back meetings from 9:00 a.m. to 7:00 p.m. with my team in the United States. Then there are times I have to take additional calls with my Bangalore team. It's the worst when it happens on a Friday."

Does this sound like your work life with no balance? After a busy day, how are you supposed to find the time for personal and family obligations? Remember that wine-tasting class you wanted to take or that piano recital or sporting event your child hoped you'd attend? Many of you are probably exhausted or can't fully enjoy personal experiences. Being at your kid's soccer match and simultaneously managing a conference call with your remote team on your handheld device does not allow you to be fully present with your family. However, to be fair, many of you are working around the clock because you love your job or think that's the expectation from your leaders. The bottom line is that your virtual teams may also be experiencing similar pains.

Global virtual burnout is on the rise. Team members who are working across geographic boundaries and time zones are jumping ship or demanding solutions for some sense of sanity and balance. It's impacting employees across the globe. United States-based employees are opting out of working with virtual teams.

"I'm an engineer, and I'm based in Pittsburgh. I've been working virtually with Asia, including the India and China offices. I've been taking calls at five o'clock in the morning for the past ten years, and I'm done. I want a regular nine-to-five job."

Global managers are more stressed than ever before. When I facilitate sessions on managing balance in a virtual world, my clients state that they struggle with the needs of managing remote teams and direct reports while maintaining balance with their personal lives. In a recent training session, 70 percent of the attending directors and managers who oversaw global teams felt like they and their employees did not have proper work-life balance. There is a direct link between work-life balance and productivity.

Consider some of the questions I present in my training sessions to global teams:

Are you setting realistic expectations for your global teams working in different time zones?

A team I interviewed in the United States rotated its meeting schedule on a monthly basis so that they would share the burden of the early-morning and late-evening calls with their team in Bangalore. Plus, they set a rule that neither team would be obligated to attend a meeting after ten o'clock at night.

Would your team benefit from flexible work hours?

A client in India I coached said he was thrilled when his manager approved a flex schedule that allowed him to be with his family from five until eight in the evening and then continue working with clients in different time zones from home.

Survey your team to find out what might create a better work-life balance for them.

A manager was not aware that traffic jams in Bangalore were one of the top factors for stress among employees. By allowing employees to work flex shifts around traffic-jam hours, he saw a significant increase in employee morale, well-being, and productivity.

The four traits of a growing number of employees in India today—I won't be stereotyped, I'm more than a paycheck, I'm loyal to myself, and I'm experiencing burnout—have a hefty impact on retention. Tomorrow's Indian workforce is definitely interested in financial rewards, but they are skeptical of the notion of lifetime employment. To stick around, they want monetary rewards and work experiences that provide a personal and immediate sense of job satisfaction.

The following chapters explain the top challenges in retaining exceptional talent. Each chapter includes a checklist of practical solutions to consider as part of your leadership strategy for retaining high-performing talent in India.

# Indian Corporate Structure

For decades, decisions in India were based on one's title and rank. Status and position defined manager-employee relationships. Within many institutions and organizational structures, characterizing a boss as a peer or a colleague may have been viewed as insubordination. The traditional hierarchical structures are changing because of the influence of socioeconomic reforms and the presence of foreign enterprises.

According to Cisco, "Traditional hierarchies in growth regions are slowly but surely shifting to a less authoritative and more collaborative model."[14] There are a few reasons for this in India. First, the business cultures from around the globe have melded, creating unique twenty-first-century business customs that constitute an alignment between Western management standards and traditional Indian business practices. The concepts of staff empowerment, gender equality, and autonomous work environments that have been part of the average Western worker's DNA have trickled into Indian corporate environments. Concepts like rank and title, which once determined the importance of "authoritative" management and pay based on seniority rather than performance, are dissipating. Managers, especially in international organizations, are transforming their methods of supervision to involve a less micromanagement style of leadership.

Second, a large percentage of employees entering the workforce, especially in large cities across India, is fueling a move toward autonomous work styles.

This outcome is based on the new generation's need for individuality. The idea is permeating their work lives and their personal lives. Prior to globalization, the average young person in India lived with family until marriage. This was due to family traditions and economic factors. Presently, many young professionals are moving to larger cities for educational and employment opportunities and have the financial freedom to live independently. Acceptance of moving out of the family home before marriage is slowly growing in large cities.

This, combined with the demand for skilled workers, is providing the latest generation to have the confidence to insist on workplaces where they can operate autonomously. They require work situations that do not confine them to the constraints of a strict hierarchy. Managers have to think differently about their staff. Those who were once heavily influenced by the traditional top-down management standards are realizing that they have to adjust to retain their employees while not jeopardizing the balance across generations of workers. Even with the shift, we cannot take for granted that the mature workforce is still somewhat entrenched in rigid hierarchies, especially in local companies and state entities. Just because incoming staff is more autonomous and hierarchies are becoming less rigid, it doesn't mean the chains of command no longer exist. In certain instances, hierarchies do still exist and cannot be taken for granted.

I discussed hierarchy and autonomy with an Indian manufacturing executive at a Fortune 500 company based in India. Here's a summary of what she told me: In Indian manufacturing organizations, rank and title define your position. When she shakes someone's hand in a first meeting, she wants to know his or her rank and how much power the person has. People have to maintain their status in the organization and define their reputations. The concept is called *Shaan*, which means dignity or honor. However, things are changing quickly, especially in urban corporate settings in Bangalore where some of her staff sits. Her young team of engineers is empowered. They prefer a hands-off approach, which is not typical of traditional Indian business. In her case, even though hierarchy is respected, she and the local leadership give her team the authority to be a part of the decision-making process.

If you're a manager with a team in India, the first thing you need to assess is the type of hierarchical structure you'll be dealing with. Because you may be part of a geographically dispersed team, you may not have access to understanding how rank, title, and power are defined on the ground at your operations in India. Assumptions may be made about who has the power to authorize a work process. I often hear about collaborative projects breaking down because senior managers have not approved the workflow. You may not be privy to who's in charge, and there may be a lack of transparency regarding hierarchical dynamics. Understanding who the key players are should be a priority. Getting your hands on an organizational chart is a great first step, but it can be tricky. Here's a lesson learned solution from one of my Chicago-based clients.

"In India, reputation is everything. The truth is often hidden because no one in the system wants to lose face or tarnish his or her reputation. In order to manage risk and failure, leaders hold on tight to information. Once a business relationship has been built, transparency can begin. Establishing rank first and then an opportunity to network and connect with your counterparts will lead to information disclosure."

As a manager, you'll have to balance the new and traditional. Do not underestimate the significance of authority and its impact on your end results. Your employees may give the impression that they are completely autonomous, but they may require leadership, a well-defined chain of command, and clear processes. Don't assume you can have a completely hands-off approach with your team. An employee's desire to work independently should not generate an absence of leadership: autonomy does not equal anarchy.

One of my Wall Street investment-banking clients was expanding her global role to include a team in Mumbai. As her coach, I advised her to implement a plan to establish the most important component of her success, which would be her authority. The steps I recommended to her are part of the following checklist. I hope it will help you implement a plan to empower yourself and your staff in India.

Indian Corporate Structure Checklist

- Have a clear understanding of the chain of command and who the decision makers are in your Indian operations. Awareness of the expectations of those in authority will alleviate any misunderstandings or process slowdowns that could arise from bypassing key decision makers.

- Obtain an organizational chart of the divisions with which you'll be partnering. You may have to do some digging. With Shaan, not all your business partners may want to be transparent.

- To obtain an organizational chart of your internal partners, the internal company database is a good place to start, but double-check to make sure it's up to date. Your HR staff in India and LinkedIn could also be excellent resources.

- If your observations indicate that the environment you'll be working with is not hierarchical, then proceed as you normally would with your home team. However, if hierarchy and rank are important, you should establish roles and define procedures.

- Start at the top. Get leadership at your end to clarify roles and expectations with the India management team.

- Another way to define and establish rank is to set up a conference call or videoconference before the start of the project to establish trust by defining individual roles in the working relationship.

- The female labor force in the traditionally male-dominated professional sector is slowly but surely on the rise. For example, women are closing the education gap. They represent 45.9 percent of all enrolled undergraduate students in India.[15]

- For female leaders managing teams in India, it is important to establish your authority. State how you fit into the scheme of the organizational structure by stating your rank, title, and expectations.

- Some of the senior leadership in India may want periodic updates. Establish how often you should connect with them. Would they like to be included in all the meetings? Do they prefer weekly or biweekly e-mail updates or conference calls?

- Make sure you keep your team accountable—and be sure they stick to their commitments. Your teams in India may give you the impression that they have the power, but in certain cases, only their leadership can enforce a process. Make sure senior leaders are signing off on the mutually agreed upon project processes in order to maintain time lines and deliverables.

- Our Indian satisfaction index indicates that 80 percent of all employees felt the working relationship was just as important as the assignment or business process. Continue building trusting relationships by having informal moments and get-togethers with key members via teleconference.

4 Managing Attrition

Attrition: a reduction in the number of employees or participants that occurs when people leave because they resign, retire, etc., and are not replaced.
—Merriam-Webster Dictionary

A McKinsey Quarterly research study titled "How Multinationals Can Attract the Talent They Need" highlights that companies will have a difficult time achieving their global ambitions if they cannot attract, retain, and excite tomorrow's employees.[16] Even though the global growth economies have matured, attrition among new hires and talented employees is a still a top challenge for managers with global teams in growth regions like India. The top three reasons include supply and demand of talent, especially those with highly specialized technical skills, lucrative sign-on and compensation packages, and guaranteed growth opportunities, including continued learning and technical training. These challenges are forcing leaders to redefine their recruiting and retention strategies, especially in technology- and engineering-related roles.

For Fortune 500 companies on-boarding information technology and engineering staff in India, the average turnover rates in the first year of employment are between 15 percent and 25 percent. Even though the level of attrition has tapered off since the 2008 recession, it is still a major concern in industries where high-level technical skills are required.

For example, in information technology, several factors influence attrition:

- IT firms have slower growth due to limited revenue growth than traditional businesses do, preventing IT firms from having better pay increases.

- Experienced workers are preferring to join next-generation companies to learn the latest tech skills.

- Employees who have been loyal to one firm become obsolete to said firm because of their lack of newer digital skills.[17]

Recruiting and hiring international teams has caused a significant amount of angst for my clients. A manager trains a talented and qualified new hire at one of his or her satellite India locations and loses the person within six months to a year. It's an expensive loss and can be a major disruption to any organization.

A manager for a IT firm told me that the junior members of his team in India expect to be given huge amounts of responsibility in their first six months. Without the technical experience under their belts, they still want to be challenged. If my client didn't provide the right training opportunities, his team members were leaving for other technically cutting-edge organizations.

International employees are looking for "challenging and meaningful assignments that are more important than employment security," and they are looking for places to work that will allow them "the flexibility to be autonomous."[18]

Another obstacle in the way of retention is that trust has a new definition in the workplace. The past recessions and company downsizings have employees of all generations across the globe jaded. Employees feel they have to look out for themselves because they don't believe that their companies are always going to be looking out for them.

In "Are Generational Differences in Work Values Fact or Fiction? Multi-Country Evidence and Implications," Julie Cogin states, "Training and incentive programs will be the primary levers vendors will employ to attract and retain top talent."[19]

To retain global teams, successful managers today have to modify the mentality that the standard business goal-setting and annual career-planning sessions with their employees will be sufficient. Attrition in India is on the radar of international and local companies. Continuous engagement is the key language I hear successful managers use. Leaders want to know how to adjust to retain employees via the right developmental programs while making sure they are aligned with budgets and overall staffing objectives.

A *Forbes* article titled "The Career-Development Gap: Why Employers Fail to Retain Top Talent" states, "Employers are reluctant to invest in workers who may not stay long and this becomes a vicious cycle: Companies won't train workers because they might leave, and workers leave because they are not getting trained." The bottom line is that "top talent is an expensive proposition. Companies must either come up with the resources to meet up the expectations of their talented employees or constantly be in the market to replenish them."[20]

Managing attrition in India will require a well-defined set of initiatives, including training programs, which can be a challenge if leaders are reluctant to invest in continued education or funding supplemental tech skills with the fear that they will leave.

Based on the current state, managers cannot underestimate the importance of their involvement in managing attrition. If you agree, and budget constraints are your concern, your first step will be to convince reluctant leadership to invest. You will have to consider your engagement throughout the one-on-one employee on-boarding process, which will be critical to understanding their career and long-term expectations. Even though there isn't necessarily one universal solution, the following checklist provides a jumping-off point for improving the process of retaining current and future talent.

Managing Attrition Checklist

- Research why people are staying in your locations in India. Gather data on what you and the organization are doing to retain staff via online-generated surveys and one-on-one feedback discussions. Partner with the local Indian leadership team to come up with a joint strategy for data collection and analysis to address the current state of attrition.

- Surveymonkey.com is an excellent online platform that will allow you to quickly create and share results of your survey real-time.

- Discover what strategies other departments and divisions within your organization in India are using to recruit staff. Partner with your HR team and your business-unit leadership to define and create a strategy for new-hire recruitment and retention.

A banking institution in Mumbai found out via one-on-one feedback from new hires that owning an apartment is a symbol of family honor and success and one's income is directly correlated to marriage proposals, especially among young professionals in large cities like Delhi and Hyderabad. To stay competitive with the on-boarding of exceptional talent, the company implemented three initiatives: a monthly apartment fund to assist employees in saving for their housing down payment, inviting immediate family members to tour the facility, and spending more time explaining long-term growth options via internal and external training initiatives.

Does your recruitment strategy include university-sourcing initiatives?

At an aerospace engineering firm in Pune, to secure top talent before they are swept off by competitors, this global company is recruiting and signing on-boarding contracts with well-trained university students a year in advance of graduation. These are joint partnerships between the recruiting manager, the HR team in India, and top local universities.

Does your recruitment strategy in India include an employee-referral program?

IBM has a well-defined global employee referral program with a reward policy. For example, in India, to encourage recruitment from outside the company, a group of IBM employees created a LinkedIn page "to inform IBMers and their networks of the several exciting opportunities that open up periodically in our company." Employees are encouraged to refer prospective employees, and if hired, they are eligible to partake in a company bonus program. [21]

Are you involved in interviewing international staff?

In "Job Interview: The Right Question," the *Times of India* provided examples of the top questions beyond remuneration that employees are asking:[22]

1) Expectations of role being offered
2) Organizational culture, work environment, and who the immediate supervisor will be
3) What the company expects from you
4) Training and development opportunities

If you will be involved in interviewing staff, here's an important note: the resume in India is called a curriculum vitae or (CV). Don't be surprised if it's multiple pages and states the person's age and marital status. Ask your local Indian HR for support on the corporate policies you should follow regarding interviewing and local hiring guidelines.

- Stay up to speed with recruitment trends by connecting with your divisional managers and HR leadership in India and provide continuous feedback to executive leadership and stakeholders on the changing dynamics. Ask your HR specialist to keep you abreast of strategies that are being used by other organizations to attract talent.

- Is your organization utilizing recruitment and social media sites such as LinkedIn, CareerBuilder.com, and Indeed.com for your recruitment efforts in India? If not, recommend that your leadership and HR team review this as a viable recruitment solution.

5 Virtual Engagement

Lack of face time with employees is a top concern I have observed in my coaching sessions for managers with dispersed groups across the globe. The water-cooler talks and informal meetings are not going to happen. The concept of building trust and managing an employee takes on a whole new meaning when you're working virtually with your teams in India. With the geographical distance between yourself and your team, you may be measuring trust and accountability solely on accomplishment of objectives and tasks. Normally, via e-mails and conference calls, your direct report delivers the indicator that objectives are being met and processes are moving forward—and you're both satisfied with this. It may not be that simple anymore. Research of dispersed teams indicates that employees are expecting informal and human connections with their virtual leadership. This is especially true of younger workers in India, which is our continual focus.

Julie Cogin's research study on multi-country generational differences suggests that younger global generations "wanted daily feedback, interactivity, and engagement with management,"[23] and a *Harvard Business Review* article titled, "What Millennials Want from Work, Charted Across the Globe" stressed the importance of social ties in the workplace more than their Western counterparts.[24]

One client mentioned the success she has with planning one-on-one time with her team members in India. A quick call with her staff members updates her on business progress and gives her a chance to understand their individual requirements. In a fifteen-minute call, she'll cover project status, next steps, and individual feedback. She has a list of questions she asks each employee:

- How is this quarter going for you?
- What would you like to see happen in your career before the start of next quarter/the end of the year?
- Where can we improve process on this project?

After the call, she brainstorms motivators for each employee. Would Raj benefit from attending the IT conference in Mumbai this spring? Ravi is desperate for a promotion. Is there time for him to shadow a department head this month? Sunina has not received an updated computer, and her work is stunted because of this. How can I expedite swapping her PC? Now that she has the information she needs and has brainstormed ways to make her employees more effective, she can rely on her assistants to help execute the plans. Employees will benefit from these efforts, and the engagement and personal attention from their manager is invaluable.

Team collaboration and recognition have to be priorities for leaders of tomorrow. Many managers I have spoken with have realized that even though they are stretched and couldn't imagine one more item on their plates, they must consider allocating time to connect and build trust. Are you creating deliberate moments with your team? More importantly, if your teams are remote, are you taking advantage of videoconferencing tools like Cisco's Telepresence to connect? Face-to-face interaction allows you to send a message that you value your global team, and it can be a highly effective collaborative tool to pick up cues from body language that ordinarily would be not clear or transparent on a conference call or e-mail.

I had dinner with a client in New York who's a project manager for a global engineering firm. I was telling her about a seminar I was preparing on defining "global leadership trust." The subject matter got her attention, and she was eager to share a recent success she'd achieved. She managed a team of fifty employees around the world, and her division was experiencing 25 percent attrition, which was especially acute in her India office. Most of the folks she managed were senior or junior aeronautical engineers. She was having a tough time maintaining momentum on business objectives with her remote teams, especially since a large percentage were leaving within six months for opportunities elsewhere. In some cases, they were leaving for their competitors. They had a strict deadline and were behind schedule. She decided to videoconference with her staff in different regions to discuss and fine-tune objectives. Before discussing business, they spent five minutes getting to know each other. Getting to know her team in India "enhanced my ability to get buy-in and commitment. Connecting on a personal level is really not my style, but the return on investment paid off tenfold. Now, when I conference call or instant message the team, they're there for me and ready to work." Videoconferencing and building trust were excellent ways to get back on track, complete projects on time, and mitigate much of the risk involved in the virtual partnership.

My clients are experiencing great success with other communication technology in addition to videoconferencing. Most corporations have embraced desktop instant messaging as a top internal country-to-country communication tool because of the benefits of immediate connection and collaboration. Intellectual property concerns in certain industries are dissipating because companies are finding ways to protect information shared via this medium. Google's GChat, Lync Instant Messaging, and mobile apps like WhatsApp Messenger aren't necessarily distractions; they can be used to your advantage. Instant messaging means instantaneous updates.

Strong virtual engagement can boost morale and fortify productivity. Even if you have time for only one of the following recommendations for engaging virtually with your staff, you'll see immediate results.

Virtual Engagement Checklist

- Create virtual water-cooler moments via company-approved technology (videoconferencing, instant messaging, one-on-one phone chats) to connect and engage with your employees.

- Determine how your team members want to engage and adapt strategies accordingly. Extroverts may appreciate the full-on engagement, and the introverts may prefer to be left alone to focus on the work. Each will have a personal preference for engagement and communication, so discern which is the best approach. An introvert may prefer one-on-one phone calls and instant messaging, and extroverts may favor videoconferencing in either a one-on-one or group setting.

- You may not be able to physically see what your teams are doing. You can exercise a certain amount of trust, but you can also ask your employees to share their workflow process through weekly updates. This will allow you to gain a better understanding of their approaches to meeting objectives.

- Create planned moments with your remote teams on a consistent basis for informal discussions and unsolicited feedback.

  o You could open an IM group chat every morning so team members can easily bounce ideas off of one another or quickly share information.

  o Make time for informal moments to connect via teleconference or weekly calls to make sure your employees have the resources, tools, and training to be effective in their roles and in their personal goals and aspirations. These highly impactful methods have proven to keep staff motivated, engaged, and wanting to stick around.

- Virtually celebrate successes and reward your global team members for any job well done. Send congratulatory and job-well-done e-mails or conduct one-on-one thank-you calls.

- Coordinate a virtual celebration with teams in different time zones. When it's morning in New York and late afternoon in Bangalore, the most senior leader in New York could virtually distribute certificates of accomplishment, congratulate the team, and express the company's gratitude for hard work.

- Look into whether your organization has company-approved social-networking tools similar to Facebook like Yammer and Chatter or Tibbr for employees to build internal business and social networks.

- Show concern during periods of low morale. This can be accomplished during your "pop-in" or impromptu calls with your staff. Your teams are juggling time zones, geographic distance, and multiple perspectives that can lead to challenging work environments. Those who are remote will especially appreciate that you are listening and are in tune with their processes and business needs.

- Conduct face-to-face meetings whenever possible. Observing facial expressions and body language will add a human dimension to your communication.

6 Say Again?

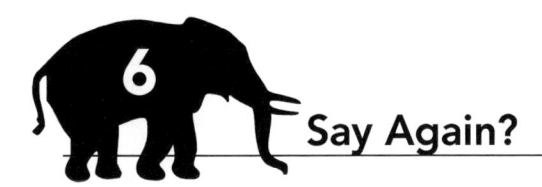

Our research at Arun Baharani Consulting indicates that the biggest barriers to global understanding on matrix teams are language and communication. In "Effective Global Communications," we explore the challenges that managers face when partnering with remote teams. Communication misunderstandings tend to include members of a team speaking different first or native languages, using regional and country-specific acronyms and idiomatic terms, language and tone misinterpretations in e-mails, and a lack of body language cues via teleconferences. These can impact the language misunderstandings and disconnects in global partnerships. An additional India-specific example I often hear is that managers are frequently walking away from virtual meetings with their partners without clearly understanding the objectives and expectations. This breakdown occurs when global managers do not ask for language clarification to avoid embarrassing themselves and their Indian counterparts, which can lead to missed deadlines and frustration.

How you share and disseminate information virtually with our remote employees is a critical and important step toward successfully building team trust. Jason Fried is a cofounder of Basecamp, a company that builds collaboration software. In an article from *Wired*, he stated, "Communication is often really subtle. When you see a chat or an e-mail, being able to picture someone helps you connect the dots."[25] He recommends face-to-face contact that reveals nonverbal cues that workers in the same office may take for granted. I've discussed the benefits of videoconferencing in previous chapters, but I want to reiterate it in regard to bridging language barriers. Body language and facial cues are important parts of effective communication. Your ability to utilize the appropriate tools for avoiding "lost-in-translation" moments will help you avoid backtracking and wasted time for your workflow process.

For effective two-way communication, the first question a manager should ask is how much time will be required for a meeting or virtual engagement. If it's a quick turnaround request, then e-mail or instant message could suffice. However, a longer-term engagement that requires project planning, training, or employee development and coaching could require another set of technological tools to include videoconferencing or desktop screen sharing.

As stated in the previous chapter, we are fortunate that today's technological tools for communicating across the globe are getting more advanced and connectivity is less of an issue. For example, utilizing Cisco's telepresence during a global videoconference team building session I facilitated for a client in New York City with participants in Chicago, London, Frankfurt, and Bangalore worked seamlessly. Each location had approximately four participants, and the technology for the three-hour training with individuals in geographically dispersed locations worked perfectly. During the majority of the session, the distance really did not matter. It's a great tool, but managers must maximize the benefits of these tools.

Too often, my clients assume that all employees will be fluent in English since it tends to be the official language for international business. That is a misconception that leads to most of the communication failures I've witnessed in global team partnerships. Long-distance language issues cause angst and impatience. The best advice I can share is the value of patience. To resolve any language and communication misunderstandings, you must have a strategically sound approach for the individual needs of the global audience you are managing. Taking the time to add the following three steps will significantly help your process.

Step One: To avoid lost-in-translation blunders, ask open-ended questions to allow for a "deep dive" into the information you seek. Here are some questions you can ask to uncover information.

- What more can you share?
- Please share an example.
- What are the steps you would consider?

Listen carefully to what is being said and summarize what you have heard. Use the information you have collected and confirm with your employee or business partner that you are both on the same page.

Step Two: As location is to real estate, visual is the key to your global communication success. With your remote teams, you may have limited time to clarify the spoken word—or you may not want to embarrass yourself or your colleague when information is not clear or completely understood. A visual tool can be a tremendous benefit to help you in your communication process. A spreadsheet, PowerPoint, or e-mail with a bulleted summary can give your global team a point of reference for improved clarity.

Step Three: Be patient. Geographic boundaries and time zones may require you to utilize an approach you are not accustomed to in your information-sharing and information-gathering processes. If your colleague's primary language is different than yours, then all parties in the process should be patient and tolerant.

Here are some additional recommendations to address regarding communication techniques.

Say Again? Checklist

- Be patient with business partners and employees whose primary language is not English by avoiding the use of slang, jargon, acronyms, and idiomatic terms.

- Manage inclusion by making sure all team members are being heard. Your ability to engage the valuable perspectives each team member brings to the table is vital for building trust.

- Learn how to pronounce the names of your partners. Ask for help with how to pronounce their names. If you receive an e-mail and are unfamiliar with the name, do not make the blunder of assuming gender. Do not write e-mails to your colleagues to ask if they are male or female. That would be a major faux pas. Instead, try googling their first names. Most names are listed with information on origin, roots of names, and phonetic spellings.

- It is critical to utilize visual aids whenever possible (spreadsheets, shared drives, PowerPoints, and webinars).

- Send a written agenda in advance of your meeting with a specific outline of objectives and attach a set of ground rules regarding meeting protocol. After every meeting, follow up with a concise e-mail on deliverables.

- For long-term collaborative projects, utilize and maximize video-conferencing for project planning, project updates, and coaching opportunities.

- Silence may indicate that people are processing the information. Be patient and don't rush.

- Avoid humor since it may not translate to those who aren't privy to regional and country-specific jokes. If you plan on utilizing humor to break the ice in the beginning of a call, I recommend explaining the context of your joke.

- Explain business or intercompany acronyms. Create a document listing all the acronyms and definitions that your team needs to know. Distribute the list to both teams so they have a quick reference. For Walt Disney Company employees, WDI for is the acronym to the department called Walt Disney Imagineering.

ID# Coaching for Success

In my recent work with executives from India, I've learned that many prospective entry-level hires ask, "How long will it take for me to be promoted into a management role?" In Cisco's "Transitioning to Workforce 2020" study, all Gen Y respondents in countries, including Brazil, China, India, and Mexico, listed career development as the number one driver for retention.[26]

A Towers Watson study looked at critical factors for employee retention by country, including Brazil, Canada, China, Germany, India, Mexico, the United Kingdom, and the United States. That study found career development and leadership were motivators valued above pay and rewards in practically all these countries.[27] A PricewaterhouseCoopers survey of 4,300 college graduates from forty-four countries rated training and development as the most highly valued company benefit.[28]

These studies deliver a clear message: Young employees require career-development coaching. In India, as opposed to previous generations, the new generation of workers has spent their entire lives in an economic system that has sustained healthy growth and wealth, and they are expecting the same for themselves. They are continually striving for better jobs with better pay. Too often, employees are trying to make this jump before they are ready.

Managers are frustrated with employees who are demanding career jumps (aka promotions to manager level) without the proper managerial skills and required technical training for the career move. A manager has to help the employee slow down and obtain the proper skill sets. This is where a manager's ability to coach is crucial. The managers who are keeping employees focused on developmental goals and defined career paths are the ones who are able to preserve qualified staff. The experts in the field are finding that coaching is quickly becoming a prerequisite skill for leaders with global reach.

Julie Cogin's study in the *Journal of Human Resources Management* found three distinct management style preferences among young international workers:[29]

1) They want daily feedback and thrive on new challenges
2) They perform best when abilities are identified and matched with challenging work and stretch goals.
3) They demand flexibility (moving from project to project, position to position, department to department, and location to location).

Managers who are juggling multiple projects may not be comfortable with the process or have the time in their busy schedules to dedicate to coaching employees who are sitting in remote locations. It may not be top of mind, and—depending on the manager—it may not necessarily be a priority. Additionally, managers may not feel as though they possess the skills to be effective coaches.

Coaching is a learned skill that doesn't necessarily come naturally to all leaders, and it requires time and energy to coach effectively. I highly recommend enrolling in a leadership-coaching class. Your company may offer one internally. If not, you may benefit from working with a global-management training organization.

One of the sessions my company facilitates is "Coaching the Next Generation of Workers in a Global Environment." I've conducted this session in one-on-one sessions and for groups of managers. The objectives of the session are enabling leaders to develop coaching skills to demonstrate that they have their employees' best interests in mind and encouraging their staffs to focus on building the long-term competencies required to be successful managers. Managers leave the sessions with the skills to provide constructive criticism and feedback on performance and employee career goal-setting strategies. In the sessions, managers learn to incorporate coaching questions into their career-coaching sessions with their staffs.

- What are your employees' career goals and why?
- What are their immediate workplace challenges?
- Do they recognize their own potential for growth?
- How do they define reward and recognition?
- What career-growth steps will help them reach their career goals?

During the sessions, I also introduce the idea of coaching with empathy and compassion. The program stresses that being a compassionate manager is not a negative attribute; it is a healthy management technique that can help improve team engagement, employee productivity, and long-term profitability. A University of New South Wales study with 5,600 people from seventy-seven organizations found compassion and empathy to be key attributes for leaders. "The ability of leaders to spend time and effort developing and recognizing their people, welcoming feedback, including criticism, and fostering cooperation among staff" was "the single greatest influence on profitability and productivity within an organization."[30]

Even though there are no guarantees that career-development initiatives will retain the best and the brightest staff, I've witnessed in my consulting work that the companies going above and beyond to create coaching and developmental initiatives in India are seeing a return on the investment by retaining their staff members. SHRM (the Society for Human Resources Management) predicts that replacing a salaried employee can cost a business an average of six to nine months in salary.[31] For a manager making $40,000 a year, that can equate to $20,000 or $30,000 in recruiting and training.[32] Instead of leaving during new-hire orientation or within six months, these initiatives could encourage employees to stay the average job tenure of 4.6 years and assist the company in avoiding the escalating costs of attrition and on-boarding replacement hires.[33]

Are staff-coaching initiatives part of your leadership agenda? If not, you can coach your staff toward career growth and success.

Coaching for Success Checklist

- Identify the number of staff members who may require career coaching as a prerequisite to their success at your global locations.

- For your remote India staff, tailor the coaching process to each individual employee by building a scheduled ongoing coaching relationship via one-on-one calls or videoconferencing.

- Build and develop your own coaching skills via your company's management training programs or an external management-training course.

- The coaching process will require you to be motivated and to set aside time and energy to administer. Effectively time-manage your development goals for your employees by setting realistic expectations for yourself and your staff.

- Encourage employees to reach out to you to schedule coaching or hold regular "open office hours" in which they can sign up for coaching.

- Assist your staff in identifying career-development goals by helping them create and maintain time-specific action plans. Set goals for three, six, nine, and twelve months, and then break these goals down into actions.

- Recommend coaching and apprenticeship programs at your company's global locations. Provide short-term assignments for high-performing employees to gain international exposure and coaching moments with senior leaders at company international locations. A fast-track junior scientist with a global pharmaceutical company in India was sent to train on an important technology-transfer initiative. As part of the program, the employee received management-skills coaching from a designated senior leader. After the three-month assignment, the employee returned with a newfound loyalty and strong desire to continue her career with the company.

- Operate from a place of empathy and compassion during your coaching efforts. Your ability to listen, be open, and fully engage may provide your employees the opportunity to discover their potential.

- Follow-up is the key to your coaching success. Here are the steps you should consider:

1) Make coaching a part of your routine by making sure you have ongoing scheduled meetings with your employees.

2) Document employee progress with well-defined notes. This will allow you to formulate and articulate your thoughts during feedback meetings.

3) Observe signs of growth by communicating periodic feedback, including growth, by giving specific examples. Include feedback if you are observing behaviors that you find contrary to the coaching-growth agreements between you and your staff members.

4) Provide immediate feedback when your employees show signs of growth or display behaviors that are contrary to agreed-upon growth opportunities.

8 Work-Life Balance

Economic downturns and job security uncertainties have required many of us to work feverishly to keep our jobs. Many leaders expect employees to be connected around the clock. The last thing we say good night to may not be our spouse or partner, but our glued-to-the-hip laptop or smartphone. Wasn't technology supposed to help us juggle our responsibilities and make our lives simpler? The biggest problem is that you can be accessed anywhere at any time of day. The 24/7 connectivity has turned many of us into virtual workaholics. Some of us may thrive in this new work reality, but the truth of the matter is that global employee-burnout levels are on the rise.

According to a 2015 study by Regus Group of more than twenty-two thousand people in one hundred countries, 53 percent reported being closer to burnout than they were five years ago.[34] In another study on the relationship between hours worked and productivity, John Pencavel of Stanford University noted that employee productivity and output fell sharply after a fifty-hour workweek and long hours were connected to absenteeism and turnover.[35]

Brian Robinson, a professor at the University of North Carolina at Charlotte and the author of *Chained to the Desk*, states that the inability to bring balance to your life and working around the clock could negatively impact a marriage and lead to poor exercise and eating habits.[36] Even with such evidence to prove its importance, work-life balance can be a hard sell to executives, especially in India where the culture of "hard work" is intrinsically connected to one's personal family and business reputation. An American survey indicates 98 percent of executives log on to work e-mail at night and on weekends, and it's tenfold with Indian executives.[37] To dismiss issues with work-life balance—regardless of geographic location—many leaders say, "The job needs to get done, so figure it out," "We have strict deadlines and need to manage time effectively no matter what," or "We're a global company with demanding clientele who cannot wait. We cannot afford to lose the business."

In the last couple of years, I have seen a rise in Indian organizations seeking solutions to work-life balance for their employees. This is a reaction to many employees experiencing burnout, which can create low morale, employment dissatisfaction, higher rates of absenteeism, and gaps in virtual productivity.

An international senior leader with an engineering team in Pune said, "I've learned to set very strict boundaries. My team in India knows that e-mails on Sundays are not welcome. We all need a day to decompress. We all want to spend time with family and friends. The boundaries benefit me too—not just my employees. Plus, the last thing I want is an unhealthy, unhappy, and unproductive team."

A manager with a pharmaceutical-research-operations group in India shared her story during a session I facilitated in Bangalore. She reported to a director in the United States who wasn't aware of her commuting time. She got a low rating in her performance evaluation in the "commitment to the job" category. During her review, she explained that she had to catch public transportation, which took an average of two hours and impeded on taking evening calls with her global colleagues. Her director understood and adjusted her schedule without hesitation. She now works from home two days a week, which allows her the flexibility to take late-afternoon calls with her American counterparts and spend quality time with her family.

As a manager, think about your stance on work-life balance. Is work-life balance something you value and incorporate into your managerial practices? Do you push your team to deliver regardless of what's happening in their personal lives? Do you need some work-life balance? Do your employees in India need it? Maybe you feel it's not even a concept that's realistic in today's frenetic, high-demand work environment. Perhaps you and your senior leaders don't require work-life balance, but your global staff might.

A *Harvard Business Review* study titled "Manage Your Work, Manage Your Life" identified the top three areas for leaders to consider for a healthy work-life balance for themselves before they tackle those of their teams.[38]

- *Defining success for yourself.* What are your strategies for work-life balance?

- *Managing technology.* Are you realistic about your business and personal expectations in a 24/7 world?

- *Building support networks.* Do you have a support system to help you manage your personal and professional life?

Does it matter—or are we spending too much time coddling people? By not adapting to the new worker expectations, does one face the prospects of losing or failing to attract top talent? Can a shift in management thinking on long-term productivity strategies and leadership guidance help solve and alleviate long-term repercussions like losing perfectly good people to another organization?

In general, current expectations for employees everywhere are long hours and long workweeks. It's highly unlikely that the pace and intensity will change anytime soon, which means leaders should be thinking of overall work-life balance activities to support a more resilient workforce. The global phenomenon we have to keep in mind is that today's young workers are not driven only by pay but also by the satisfaction of work-life balance. You need to think about three steps in order to gauge what work-life balance means to your Indian teams and potentially come up with an approach to influence your organization's take on work-life balance.

- Step 1: Identify your own stance on work-life balance.

- Step 2: Uncover the work-life balance needs of your staff through surveys or one-on-one feedback.

- Step 3: Come up with a game plan by outlining ways to balance business expectations and the personal needs of your staff. You may not be able to change the corporate culture overnight, but your actions can transform the productivity culture of your team or business unit. Being cognizant of the individual needs of your employees can have a positive impact and potentially influence long-term corporate change.

Here are some further recommendations regarding work-life balance.

Work-Life Integration Checklist

- Are you an advocate for work-life balance for your teams? If not, measuring employee feedback regarding burnout and stress should be your first step. Gathering data via one-on-one feedback meetings and informal online surveys on work hours versus productivity could help you determine your long-term strategy. Waggl.com has a great online tool to help you capture immediate feedback for quick actionable solutions.

- Minimize stress and maximize productivity by setting up rules of healthy nonengagement. Be explicit to your team on when and how they should disengage. One leader I advised initiated Sunday as an "e-mail-free day" and "periodic informal nonwork lunches."

- During high-stress deadlines and crunch times, build in downtime for yourself and your teams at your remote locations so employees can take some time with their family, friends, and personal passions and interests. A manager with a team absorbed in a heavy, around-the-clock, seven-days-per-week schedule to meet a global project deadline allowed each team member one day to recuperate each week. That person was free from engaging in calls and e-mails for twenty-four hours. The days would rotate to provide all team members with a full day off.

- Encourage your Indian staff to take their vacations. They'll get time to chill and come back happy, reenergized, and ready to perform.

- Make sure that staff members who are on vacation are "off duty" and really on vacation. They should not feel any pressure to answer e-mails or get on conference calls.

- Advise employees that not taking a vacation and trying to outshine others by working around the clock is counterproductive to the entire team's health.

- As a manager, seek more balance for yourself and your remote teams by leaving the office early one night per week.

- As a manager, are you encouraging good habits that will impact your overall attitude and boost your energy level? Try a walk at lunchtime or healthier food and drink options. A manager in Mumbai lets her team hit the company gym to reenergize. Yoga and five-minute meditations can help with stress.

- Don't be afraid to hire a life-balance coach for you or members of your staff to help you find anti-burnout solutions.

9 Managing Time Zones

You arrive at your workstation early on a Monday morning in New York and are greeted by a slew of e-mails and IMs from your Hyderabad partners who are coming to the end of their day. They're eager to pass along information to you and receive guidance on project processes. They are informing you of a local holiday that will close their office the following day. This is all happening before you've even had a chance to taste your first cup of java. Sound familiar? Managing across time zones can be a daunting task, and it requires adaptability, strong organizational skills, and respect for all team members.

A decade ago, teams in India would bite the bullet and not state how working around the clock with multiple time zones was negatively impacting their personal lives. This was especially true in traditional and formal business cultures where employees would do whatever it took to be viewed as team players and not tarnish their reputations. Following the rules and working hard were the stereotypical cornerstones of the Indian business DNA.

We are all impacted by time zones in one way or another. Whether your call from India is making you stay late or you're missing out on family time, we are looking for creative coping mechanisms in terms of staying productive across time zones. How a manager understands the local dynamics and plans for effective workflow across time zones is the solution to overcoming productivity barriers.

In your process on finding solutions that benefit you, don't forget the specific needs of your Indian team members. They will appreciate you taking the time to ascertain the best solution for all involved. Be willing to consider each of your staff member's personal needs by sharing the time burden. For example, rotate the times of engagement. Your daily call should not always be eight o'clock in the morning in the United States and half past six in the evening in India, which is a scenario I often see. Consider scheduling half the calls at a time that's early for the Indian team. That way, your team in India won't have to consistently end their workdays so late. This healthy step can combat safety concerns and low productivity, and it can help employees balance work and personal obligations.

One manager with a team in Mumbai explained to me that he really needed his team present on update calls, but he wasn't aware of the local cultural issues impacting their productivity in India. He learned about his industry's Indian workplace safety laws that allow female staff members to opt not to work late hours on-site. He was also informed that members of his staff were dealing with heavy traffic issues with commutes upwards of two hours. He made moves to accommodate his staff. His department received the appropriate funding to have critical team players work from home for early-morning or late-evening calls. They obtained access to high-speed connections at their homes and company smartphones so their workflow and processes would be not disrupted. His staff members were happy to work in their home environments a couple days a week and avoid the hectic, painful commutes to the office.

Overcoming time-zone obstacles can improve the workflow of your Indian team.

Managing Time Zones Checklist

- Research the personal preferences of team members in regard to meeting times. Some may prefer mornings, and others may prefer evenings or nights.

- Share the time-zone burden. Rotate meeting times so one team does not always have to take calls at odd hours.

- Let your teams decide where they would prefer to take calls. They may prefer to take early-morning calls or late-night calls at home. This could mitigate stress and increase productivity.

- Make sure people's personal obligations are valued and insist on beginning and ending all meetings on time.

- For calls at odd hours, some team members may be dialing in while commuting or from home. Make sure they have their devices on mute to avoid background distractions.

- Create an agile work environment with a backup plan. If one technology—such as videoconferencing—fails, make sure you can quickly switch to another option.

- Download a world clock for reference as you accurately manage your teams in different zones. The world clock app for iPhone or Android is a great tool.

- Know the local holidays and schedule your meetings accordingly. Diwali is one of the biggest festivals for Hindus, Buddhists, Jains, and Sikhs, and employees will take time off to celebrate with their families.

10 The Hyper-Connected World

Chief technology officers who attend my consulting sessions often state that they have to seek solutions that balance IT security with constant advances in global communication and collaboration technology. For example, you may want to incorporate multiple interfacing tools like desktop-video technology and project-management software for your global collaboration. However, the tech tools may not be available at your global sites due to security risks or lack of infrastructure.

My clients in certain industries are working with previous-generation communication technology, which causes frustration for those with quicker, more efficient collaboration tools. This can heavily impact your ability to be productive with virtual teams. Is your organization evolving with the technology? Do all your teams in India have access to videoconferencing, the ability for documents to be edited by multiple people all over the world at the same time, sharing screenshots, and chatting over instant messaging? If cutting-edge technology, bandwidth, and connectivity are issues, are you utilizing your current tools of e-mailing and conference calling effectively?

Thomas Friedman said, "The simple definition of globalization is the interweaving of markets, technology, information systems, and telecommunication networks in a way that is shrinking the world from a size medium to a size small."[39] The percentage of the population using the Internet in the United States is 87.4 percent; China is at 49.5 percent, and India is at 30 percent.[40] Even though there is a disparity of users between the United States and these growth regions, Internet usage in urban areas of India and China will continue to grow at a rapid pace. The trend of smartphones as a main source of business communication has been driving a shift away from conventional computers. Today, approximately two billion people across the globe use smartphones with Internet connections, and by the end of the decade, that number will exceed six billion.[41] Deloitte's "Tech Trends" series predicts a "mobile-only" future for the global workforce.[42] Is your organization embracing the mobile work space?

The technologically interconnected world has created a generation of international citizens who are filling the "humanity gap many global workers feel in cold, impersonal e-mail chains and conference calls."[43] Facebook, YouTube, Twitter, Instagram, and blogs are ubiquitous across the globe. A 2013 study found the "majority of the new generation of workers say they carry out personal tasks during work hours. Though keen to perform well at work, it is virtually impossible for them to leave their personal lives behind, as they typically check Facebook, conduct IM chats and send and receive messages on their devices throughout the day. This is seen as a right rather than a benefit."[44] An Accenture study outlined that "45 percent of young employees globally use social networking sites at work, whether prohibited or not" with "30 percent of the research indicating that the employees don't even know if their company has a corporate IT policy."[45]

In their business and personal lives, the young global workforce is living with the latest technology—and they expect similar or more advanced tools in the workplace. The same Accenture study found that state-of-the-art technology was most important to young employees in India, and three in four consider it essential when choosing an employer."[46] Is your organization trying to keep up with tomorrow's cutting-edge tools with yesterday's technology? Does your organization frown upon employees connecting on their smartphones for personal reasons at work? Is time spent on social media outlets like LinkedIn a hindrance to collaboration—or are these connections creating an interconnected network that can enhance and impact work-related relationships and collaboration. To attract and retain tech-savvy next-generation workers, businesses with a presence in growth regions like India have to discover and utilize enterprise-tool solutions that are current and relevant. They must create long-term sustainable policies that balance security and seamless collaboration.

To understand your organization's current technological state, here are some recommendations to address:

The Hyper-Connected World Checklist

- Could you as a leader influence your business results by making sure your teams are equipped with the latest collaborative tech tools? This should be a question to consider as you engage with your global teams.

- Assess how well equipped your organization is with tech tools at your international locations.

    1) Step 1: Check in with your Indian tech department to confirm the availability of resources like bandwidth, videoconferencing tools, and desktop screen-sharing capabilities.

    2) Step 2: Check with your team to find which resources would be the most beneficial for your virtual communication and collaboration.

    3) Step 3: Form a plan and attain leadership buy in to implement the use of the agreed-upon tools.

- Does your company utilize business-friendly social networking tools like Yammer (a private social-enterprise tool for intracompany business communication that allows users to collaborate across divisions and departments)?

- Does your organization approve employees visiting sites like LinkedIn and Twitter to connect with prospective hires, vendors, clients, educational institutions, and industry organizations? Is your HR department able to access the Twitter page for the Society for Human Resources Management (SHRM) for global HR updates? If not, research if access to these sites could positively impact productivity.

- If networking sites and tools are not available to you and your teams, check if your organization is open to—and willing to invest in—such platforms.

- To stay current, does your organization incorporate regular software-system upgrades at your global locations? If not, assist with the creation of a business case to senior leaders to justify the need for such tools (noting how they would positively impact global collaboration).

- Are you encouraging your global teams to use collaboration tech tools to share insightful information on projects? A project team working on its first assignment with India could create a Wiki page listing lessons learned on a weekly basis to document best practices for future reference.

11 The Virtual Workspace

The theory that workplace design positively impacts workforce productivity is often viewed by C-suite leaders as irrelevant or cost prohibitive. Having spent multiple years in global Fortune 500 office environments, I am convinced there is a correlation between investing in office ergonomics and employee work output, creativity, and engagement.

Whether to utilize open-floor work spaces or typical cubicle-office floor plans is an ongoing debate in today's workplaces, and there is no definitive winner. Regardless of which environment you've created for your global staff, I believe it's a win-win to create an environment that uses technology and design to increase productivity. According to a *Harvard Business Review* article, "If companies can change their spaces to reflect how people work, performance improvements will follow."[47] How can your work environment impact innovation, interactions, and creativity?

Silicon Valley companies like Google and Facebook have been at the forefront of workplace design. They've conceived campuses that embrace the philosophy that well-designed spaces with easy access to technological tools for virtual collaboration will enhance performance and productivity. However, organizations are questioning whether these approaches are just another new tech-generation fad.

Scott Birnbaum, a vice president of Samsung Semiconductor, states their American headquarters "is really designed to spark, not just collaboration, but that innovation you see when people collide."[48] Birnbaum also suggests that by "combining the emerging data with organizational metrics such as total sales or number of new product launches, we can demonstrate a work space's effect on the bottom line and then engineer the space to improve it."[49] This is clearly the ROI selling point to corporate. Companies like Samsung are investing in trends that ultimately are the foundations of future corporate-environment design.

The technology we use at work has changed so it would make sense to adjust our office environments accordingly. Design has to incorporate a fluid and flexible work space that blends with technological tools for global-communication partnerships. One of my high-tech-manufacturing clients in the United States decided on a work space facelift at their headquarters. Small, partitioned cubicles became open floor plans with easy and quick access to conference areas with video communication tools for connecting with their virtual counterparts. Creative zones were designated throughout the building with virtual-communication equipment like videophones for brainstorming and innovative moments. Comfortable "reflection spaces" on every floor were created for employees to meditate and recharge. People could grab coffee at the strategically placed beverage stations with teleconference access that were specially designed for engaging with their global staff for quick updates and meetings. While planning the new design, the company was sensitive to introverted employees who would prefer quiet work spaces by creating noise-free and interaction-free work zones within the floor plan.

This was an example of a complete redesign, but there are ways to implement a global collaborative work environment without construction. Spare conference rooms can be dedicated as reflection spaces for meditation at certain times of the day. You can survey and find out which employees prefer quiet environments and reassign cubicle spaces accordingly. Dedicate a section of the cafeteria as a community space with couches and blackboards—and perhaps even a video game console or a pool table. Employees can hold meetings there or take breaks that allow them to recharge and sharpen their thinking. A *New York Times* article titled "To Stay on Schedule, Take a Break" states that "a growing body of evidence shows that taking regular breaks from mental tasks improves productivity and creativity—skipping breaks can lead to stress and exhaustion."[50]

This may sound far-fetched and only aimed at attracting a new generation of workers with a Silicon Valley mind-set. I disagree. Corporations are realizing that they need to step up their games when it comes to the environments they are creating for all workers. This mind-set can benefit every generation of employees in the current global workforce. All generations can recharge in the meditation room or reap the benefits of an open community space. Otherwise, I truly believe workers will continue to jump ship and look for other environments outside the current traditional corporate landscape.

How can you influence the design of your global workplaces to be more collaborative and innovative? Here are some suggestions for how to improve your work environments.

The Virtual Workspace Checklist

- Reposition your mind-set about work-space design. Think about the design of the space as an integral benefit to your bottom line versus the standard practice of inexpensively filling space with cubicles. In the long term, a well-designed space can benefit retention and productivity. To maximize the output of your global staff, accommodate their personality types by providing open spaces for the extroverts and private, enclosed work spaces for introverts.

- Collect feedback and suggestions from your Indian team to address design recommendations. Would they appreciate quiet spaces for reflection? What are their opinions on open floor plans? What are the necessary technology upgrades for international collaborations? Influence leaders to understand workplace design's positive impact on innovation and productivity.

- Survey your Indian teams to measure how conducive their work spaces are to global team meetings. Do they have teleconference equipment and easy access to conference rooms?

- Partner with leaders in India to determine if the work environments are designed with the necessary bandwidth for global collaboration.

- Create environments at your offices where people can connect and unwind. For example, an accounting firm I partnered with had a high-tech lobby with proper outlets, a lounge area, and work spaces to decompress or hold quick meetings.

- If you have limited budgets, think of easy-to-implement solutions. For example, convert rarely used lounge spaces into reflection spaces.

- Add simple design elements such as clocks with the times of your company's key international locations to reinforce the global aspect of your work.

12 Your First Step

Congratulations are in order as you've already taken a great first step in the process toward better global virtual team management by your openness to learn about attracting, managing, and retaining staff in India. Changing your mind-set is the jumping-off point. We've learned that generational workforce-behavioral changes and global diversities are more intricate than ever. A new generation of global workers is redefining how leaders have to think about their own managerial skills for effective global collaboration. Leaders who do not closely review global generational trends may eventually become obsolete.

You may be questioning why corporations suddenly have to change at a whim for the needs of a group that some consider capricious, impetuous, self-absorbed young people. Shouldn't the newcomers adapt to the systems we've established? Today's workers are a force to be reckoned with. The younger generations entering the workforce across the globe are voicing their aspirations. Because of technology, this group's goals, attitudes, and behaviors are borderless—and their expectations are impacting your bottom line. If their influence was insignificant, Fortune 500 companies would not be investing heavily in reshaping how they attract, manage, and retain staff.

If you have a global staff of young employees in India, this is not a topic that can be shelved for later consideration. To be ahead of the seismic workforce shifts that are occurring today, a radical transformation in thinking regarding corporate policies and procedures will be a requirement. This is the first step toward success in the upcoming decades.

We can change how we think about managing our global teams. The payoff will be higher productivity, better retention, and employees who don't dread coming to work in the morning. All generations have had to work for a living. It's important to find common ground in the workplace—even if it means taking the time to adjust the way we've always worked and creating a new approach to managing future generations in the workforce.

Endnotes

1. Julie Cogin, "Are Generational Differences in Work Values Fact or Fiction? Multi-Country Evidence and Implications," *The International Journal of Human Resource Management* Vol. 23. No. 11 June 2012, 2268-2294, http://www.tandfonline.com/doi/abs/10.1080/09585192.2011.610967
2. "Big Demands and High Expectations: The Deloitte Millennial Survey," *Deloitte: DTTl Global Brands and Communication*, 2014, https://www2.deloitte.com/content/dam/Deloitte/global/Documents/About-Deloitte/gx-dttl-2014-millennial-survey-report.pdf
3. Kathryn Dill, "The Best Companies for Work-Life Balance," *Forbes*, 29 Jul. 2014, http://www.forbes.com/sites/kathryndill/2014/07/29/the-best-companies-for-work-life-balance/#66408656d86a
4. IBM, "Employee Well-Being," IBM.com, http://www.ibm.com/ibm/responsibility/employee_well_being.shtml
5. Ben Waber, Jennifer Magnolfi, and Greg Lindsay, "Workspaces that Move People," *Harvard Business Review*, Oct. 2014, <https://hbr.org/2014/10/workspaces-that-move-people>
6. Henrik Bresman, "What Millennials Want from Work: Charted Across the Globe," *Harvard Business Review*, 23 Feb. 2015, <https://hbr.org/2015/02/what-millennials-want-from-work-charted-across-the-world>
7. Charles M. Blow, "The Self(ie) Generation," *The New York Times*, Mar. 7, 2014, http://www.nytimes.com/2014/03/08/opinion/blow-the-self-ie-generation.html?_r=0
8. U Anand Kumar, "Average Age of India's Population to be Around 29 in Five Years, Says Economic Report," *The New Indian Express*, Feb. 28, 2014, http://www.newindianexpress.com/nation/Average-Age-of-India's-Population-to-be-29-in-Five-Years-Says-Economic-Survey/2015/02/28/article2690829.ece

9   Rohini Pande and Moore Charity Troyer, "Why Aren't India's Women Working," *The New York Times*, Aug. 23, 2015, http://www.nytimes.com/2015/08/24/opinion/why-arent-indias-women-working.html?_r=0
10 Rohini Pande and Moore Charity Troyer, "Why Aren't India's Women Working," *The New York Times*, Aug. 23, 2015, http://www.nytimes.com/2015/08/24/opinion/why-arent-indias-women-working.html?_r=0
11 Kate Taylor, "Why Millennials Are Ending the 9 to 5," *Forbes*, Aug. 23, 2013, http://www.forbes.com/sites/katetaylor/2013/08/23/why-millennials-are-ending-the-9-to-5/
12 Charles M. Blow, "The Self(ie) Generation," *The New York Times*, Mar. 7, 2014, http://www.nytimes.com/2014/03/08/opinion/blow-the-self-ie-generation.html?_r=0
13 "Global Firms in 2020: The Next Decade of Change for Organisations and Workers," *Economist Intelligence Unit Report*, September 2010, https://www.shrm.org/research/surveyfindings/articles/documents/economist%20research%20-%20global%20firms%20in%202020.pdf
14 Cisco, "Transitioning to Workforce 2020: Anticipating and Managing the Changes that will Radically Transform Working Life in the Next Decade," 2011, http://www.cisco.com/c/dam/en_us/about/ac49/ac55/docs/Workforce_2020_White_Paper_012411.pdf
15 *Indiastat*, "State-wise Enrolment at Various Levels of Higher Education in India: Part I," 2012–2013, http://www.indiastat.com/education/6370/enrolments/6373/enrolmentinhighereducationclassesabovexii/366801/stats.aspx
16 Martin Dewhurst, Matthew Pettigrew, and Ramesh Srinivasan, "How Multinationals Can Attract the Talent They Need," *McKinsey Quarterly*, Jun. 2012, http://www.mckinsey.com/insights/organization/how_multinationals_can_attract_the_talent_they_need
17 Te Raja Seman, "Attrition on the Rise in IT Firms," *The Hindu Business Line*, Feb. 26, 2014, http://www.thehindubusinessline.com/features/smartbuy/attrition-on-the-rise-in-it-firms/article5730053.ece
18 Julie Cogin, "Are Generational Differences in Work Values Fact or Fiction? Multi-Country Evidence and Implications," *The International Journal of Human Resource Management*, Vol. 23, No. 11, Jun. 2012, 2268-2294, http://www.tandfonline.com/doi/abs/10.1080/09585192.2011.610967
19 Julie Cogin, "Are Generational Differences in Work Values Fact or Fiction? Multi-Country Evidence and Implications," *The International Journal of Human*

Resource Management, Vol. 23. No. 11 Jun. 2012, 2268-2294, http://www.tandfonline.com/doi/abs/10.1080/09585192.2011.610967

20 Panos Mourdoukoutas, "The Career-Development Gap: Why Employers Fail to Retain Top Talent." *Forbes,* 11 Jul. 2012, http://www.forbes.com/sites/panosmourdoukoutas/2012/07/11/1-career-development-gap-why-employers-fail-to-retain-top-talent/

21 LinkedIn, "Employee Referral Program," *IBM,* 2016, https://www.linkedin.com/groups/4123002/profile

22 Purnima Goswami Sharma, "Job Interview: The Right Question," *The Times of India,* 17 Jan. 2015, http://timesofindia.indiatimes.com/life-style/relationships/work/Job-interview-The-right-question/articleshow/23640381.cms

23 Julie Cogin, "Are Generational Differences in Work Values Fact or Fiction? Multi-Country Evidence and Implications," *The International Journal of Human Resource Management,* Vol. 23, No. 11, Jun. 2012, http://www.tandfonline.com/doi/abs/10.1080/09585192.2011.610967

24 Henrik Breman, "What Millennials Want from Work: Charted Across the Globe," *Harvard Business Review,* 23 Feb. 2015, https://hbr.org/2015/02/what-millennials-want-from-work-charted-across-the-world

25 Joe Brown, "Working From Home Does Not Have to Cut You Off From Humanity," *Wired,* 12 Mar. 2015, http://www.wired.com/2015/03/work-from-home/

26 "Transitioning to Workforce 2020: Anticipating and Managing the Changes that will Radically Transform Working Life in the Next Decade," *Cisco Report,* 2011, http://www.cisco.com/c/dam/en_us/about/ac49/ac55/docs/Workforce_2020_White_Paper_012411.pdf

27 "2104 Global Workforce Study." *Towers Watson Study,* August 2014, https://www.towerswatson.com/en-US/Insights/IC-Types/Survey-Research-Results/2014/08/the-2014-global-workforce-study

28 "Talent Mobility 2020 and Beyond," PricewaterhouseCoopers Study, 2012, http://www.pwc.com/gx/en/issues/talent/future-of-work/global-mobility-map.html

29 Julie Cogin, "Are Generational Differences in Work Values Fact or Fiction? Multi-Country Evidence and Implications," *The International Journal of Human Resource Management,* Vol. 23, No. 11, June 2012, http://www.tandfonline.com/doi/abs/10.1080/09585192.2011.610967

30 "The Rise of the Compassionate Leader: Should you be Cruel to be Kind," *Business Think: UNSW Business School,* 21 Aug. 2012, https://www.businessthink.unsw.edu.au/Pages/The-Rise-of-the-Compassionate-Leader--Should-You-Be-Cruel-to-Be-Kind.aspx

31 Christina Merhar, "Employee Retention: The Cost of Losing an Employee," *ZaneBenefits,* 4 Feb. 2016
32 http://www.zanebenefits.com/blog/bid/312123/Employee-Retention-The-Real-Cost-of-Losing-an-Employee
33 Christina Merhar, "Employee Retention: The Cost of Losing an Employee," *ZaneBenefits,* 4 Feb. 2016, http://www.zanebenefits.com/blog/bid/312123/Employee-Retention-The-Real-Cost-of-Losing-an-Employee
34 Justin Fox, "Sticking with the Same Job is Not Out of Style," *Bloomberg View,* 12 Jan. 2016, http://www.bloombergview.com/articles/2016-01-12/sticking-with-the-same-job-isn-t-out-of-style
35 "Majority on Brink of Stress: Office Tensions Rising but Flexible Working Provides a Solution," *Regus Report,* 7 Jan. 2015, http://press.regus.com/hong-kong/majority-on-brink-of-stress
36 Bob Sullivan, "Memo to Work Martyrs: Long Hours Make You Less Productive," *CNBC,* 26 Jan. 2015, http://www.cnbc.com/2015/01/26/working-more-than-50-hours-makes-you-less-productive.html
37 Brian Robinson, "Chained to the Desk: A Guidebook for Workaholics, Their Partners and Children and the Clinicians Who Treat Them," New York University Press, 1998, 37. "Engaging the Most Engaged, The @Work State of Mind Project," *Forbes Insights Report,* 2012, http://images.forbes.com/forbesinsights/StudyPDFs/gyroAtWorkStateofMind.pdf
38 Boris Groysberg and Robin Abrahams, "Manage Your Work, Manage Your Life," *Harvard Business Review,* March 2014, https://hbr.org/2014/03/manage-your-work-manage-your-life/ar/1
39 Thomas L. Friedman, *The World Is Flat: A Brief History of the Twenty-First Century,* Farrar, Straus, and Giroux, New York, NY.
40 "Usage and Population Statistics for Top 20 Countries," *Internet World Stats,* 2013, http://www.internetworldstats.com/top20.htm
41 Ingrid Lunden, "6.1B Smartphone Users Globally By 2020, Overtaking Basic Fixed Phone Subscriptions," *TechCrunch,* 2 Jun. 2015, http://techcrunch.com/2015/06/02/6-1b-smartphone-users-globally-by-2020-overtaking-basic-fixed-phone-subscriptions/
42 Natalie Burg, "How Technology Has Changed Workplace Communication," *Forbes/Tech,* 10 Dec. 2013, http://www.forbes.com/sites/unify/2013/12/10/how-technology-has-changed-workplace-communication/
43 Natalie Burg, "How Technology Has Changed Workplace Communication," *Forbes/Tech,* 10 Dec. 2013, http://www.forbes.com/sites/unify/2013/12/10/how-technology-has-changed-workplace-communication/

44 Consumer Labs, "Young Professionals at Work," *Ericsson Report*, April 2013, http://www.ericsson.com/res/docs/2013/consumerlab/young-professionals-at-work.pdf http://www.forbes.com/sites/unify/2013/12/10/how-technology-has-changed-workplace-communication/
45 "Jumping the Boundaries of Corporate IT: Accenture Global Research on Millennials' use of Technology," Accenture Report, 2012, http://nstore.accenture.com/technology/millennials/global_millennial_generation_research.pdf
46 "Jumping the Boundaries of Corporate IT: Accenture Global Research on Millennials' use of Technology," Accenture Report, 2012, http://nstore.accenture.com/technology/millennials/global_millennial_generation_research.pdf
47 Ben Waber, Jennifer Magnolfi, and Greg Lindsay, "Workplaces That Move People," *Harvard Business Review*, Oct. 2015, https://hbr.org/2014/10/workspaces-that-move-people
48 Ben Waber, Jennifer Magnolfi, and Greg Lindsay, "Workplaces That Move People." *Harvard Business Review* Oct. 2015, https://hbr.org/2014/10/workspaces-that-move-people
49 Ben Waber, Jennifer Magnolfi, and Greg Lindsay, "Workplaces That Move People," *Harvard Business Review*, Oct. 2015, https://hbr.org/2014/10/workspaces-that-move-people
50 Phyllis Korkki, "To Stay on Schedule, Take a Break," *The New York Times*, 16 Jun. 2012, http://www.nytimes.com/2012/06/17/jobs/take-breaks-regularly-to-stay-on-schedule-workstation.html?_r=0

About the Author

Arun Baharani is the founder and principal at Arun Baharani Consulting in New York City and has worked in the multicultural-consulting field for more than fifteen years.

Before launching his career as a global-management consultant, Mr. Baharani worked as a CNN newsroom writer and international protocol attaché, providing guidance on cultural etiquette, language translations, and global-protocol debriefs to senior newsroom executives. He represented CNN as an international protocol attaché to world leaders during the 1996 Olympic Games. Mr. Baharani also worked as a multicultural-project leader at the Walt Disney Company and led cross-cultural business strategies for company-wide multicultural initiatives.

Currently, Mr. Baharani's main focus has been to provide executive coaching and consulting to Fortune 500 clients and United States government agencies. Mr. Baharani's expertise includes preparing international teams with the cross-cultural competencies necessary for business success in Asia.

Mr. Baharani speaks French, Italian, Dutch, Chinese (Cantonese), Hindi, Sindhi, and English. He's had extensive international experience as an expatriate, living and working in various countries across the globe, including the Netherlands, Italy, India, and China (Hong Kong).

During Mr. Baharani's foreign assignments, he played an active role in the international chapters of the American Chamber of Commerce and other international business organizations. He's also involved in multicultural and diversity initiatives both professionally and personally. Mr. Baharani currently splits his time between New York City and Mumbai.

Website: arunbaharaniconsulting.com
Twitter: @arunbaharani